STAYING POWER

Four Keys to a Long-Lasting Marriage

Maurice & Vivian Banks

ISBN-13: 9798323012077

Self-Published by Maurice and Vivian Banks - DBA 'Vivian Banks Designs'

Email: vbandmb4ever@gmail.com

All Scripture is given by inspiration of God. All Scripture is taken from The King James Version of the Bible, except where noted. The King James Version present on the Bible Gateway matches the 1987 printing. The KJV is public domain in the United States.

Scriptures taken from the Holy Bible, New International Version ®, NIV®. Copyright © 1973, 1978, 1984, 2011 by Biblica, Inc. ™ Used by permission of Zondervan. All rights reserved worldwide. www.zondervan.com The "NIV" and "New International Version" are trademarks registered in the United States Patent and Trademark Office by Biblica, Inc. TM

Scripture quotations are taken from the Amplified ® Bible (AMP). Copyright © 2015 by The Lockman Foundation. Used by permission. www.lockman.org

Four Keys
to a
Long-Lasting
Marriage

Marriage may sometimes seem like an uphill battle, but the battle has already been won. Keep climbing!

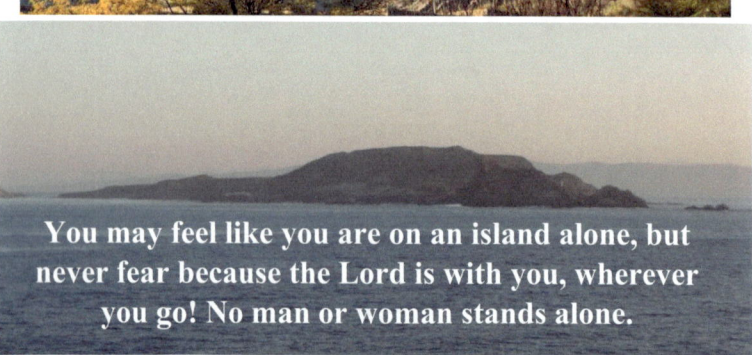

You may feel like you are on an island alone, but never fear because the Lord is with you, wherever you go! No man or woman stands alone.

Storms, hurricanes, and cyclones can cause a variety of hazards, and bring some destruction, but they also redistribute heat through precipitation. Storms are nature's way of rebalancing order on Earth. The rainbow appears after the storm when the sun is at the right angle and the sun's rays pass through the raindrops. There is a bright side somewhere! Keep standing even though some things have been washed away.

Table of Contents

Dedication

First and foremost, this book is dedicated to:

Our Heavenly Father, who ordained marriage, *"Therefore shall a man leave his father and his mother, and shall cleave unto his wife: and they shall be one flesh"* (Genesis 2:24)

My wife, who is my love, constant support, and encourager. She always does her best to help me and has helped me gain knowledge in many areas. I am grateful for her unselfishness and the gift she is to me from God. We are a united team; her love and understanding have been invaluable over our 53 years together. Every morning, her singing and praising God uplift my spirit and inspire me to start the day with gratitude. From your loving husband, Maurice.

My husband, who is an incredible person who loves, encourages, and supports me every day. He is my partner in everything and a true blessing in my life. Even though I tease him about robbing the cradle, he is the husband of my youth – my friend, lover, helper, and buddy – and I am grateful for every moment we have had together. Maurice was not always the man of my dreams, but he has become the man of my heart. He is a gem in the rough, and I cannot imagine my life without him. He has always been my knight in shining armor, even if there were times when I wanted to take his armor and clunk him with it! Jokes aside, he has always been there for me, whether it was helping me dress the children for school or church or sharing in the household chores. He would wash the dishes, clean the house, and do whatever he could to make our house a home. I am truly blessed to have him in my life. We have faced many trials and hardships, but with the help of God, we have overcome them. Throughout these challenging times, we have learned to love and support each other, always keeping our faith in the Lord and His Word. We have grown together and strengthened our bond by relying on our faith. What the Lord has joined together, no one can separate! With love, Vivian.

"For we are members of His body, of His flesh and of His bones. For this cause shall a man leave his father and mother and be joined to his wife, and the two shall become one flesh. This is a great mystery, but I speak concerning Christ and the church. Nevertheless let every one of you in particular so love his own wife as himself, and let the wife see that she reverence her husband." (Ephesians 5:30-33)

Introduction

Congratulations on reading our book, *Staying Power - Four Keys to a Long-Lasting Marriage*! We are honored to share our secrets to a successful marriage with all of you. We have been blessed to celebrate our 53rd wedding anniversary, and we are grateful to have had real-life experiences that kept our marriage and bond strong. We understand that marriage is not always easy, but with hard work, dedication, love, and prayer, it can be a fulfilling and happy union. It all starts with dating and building a solid foundation that will withstand the test of time.

In our book, we share what we have found to be four major keys that have aided us in having a long-lasting marriage: communication, money, sex, and relationship. These keys are crucial to building a solid foundation in a marriage and neglecting them can lead to a broken and crumbling union. We will provide insights from both the dating and marriage perspectives, but our primary focus is to help couples cultivate these keys and make their marriage last.

Although we are not board-certified experts or possess a "Marriage and Family Therapy" license with a master's or doctoral degree, we can give you our honest opinions based on what we have learned from our own experiences that are verified by life. We graduated from the "school of hard knocks" with significant clinical practice and many quarter hours. We welcome you to join us on our journey and learn from the experiences we share about ourselves and others.

To those who may be struggling in their marriage, please do not be discouraged. A successful marriage requires the cooperation of both partners. If either the husband or the wife is unwilling to work together and make an effort for the marriage to succeed, then it may be best to take notice of patterns and practices and leave the marriage in peace. Although it is not in God's perfect will for marriages to end, it may be in His permissive will. Physical, psychological, or emotional abuse, infidelity, forsaking marriage for other things, or a hardened heart are signs that separation may be necessary unless instructed otherwise by the Lord.

For those contemplating marriage, we encourage you to learn from the mistakes of others and avoid repeating past failures. You are welcome to use any examples in this book to help you navigate this diverse test of endurance. If you are ready, your marriage, honeymoon, and life together can be rewarding and long-lasting. Work together to make it last. Enjoy the ups and downs, challenges, and accomplishments that come your way. By reading this book, you may be able to build a **long–lasting** and enjoyable marriage.

If your marriage is at the point of termination, move forward and find peace. Remember, God is your help and strength, and He will never leave you or forsake you.

PART I: Staying Power

Marriage is not a sprint but a marathon and ministry that should last over time. Unlike a sprint, which is a short and fast race, marriage is more like a marathon, which is a long-distance race. When you enter into the marriage marathon, you are in it to win it. However, we as humans often complicate things and deviate from God's intended plan for marriage. The only perfect marriage is in Christ when we meet the Bridegroom in person. As humans, we strive to achieve perfection until then. Although we strive for perfection, we may encounter difficulties and challenges, however, solutions can be found in Christ if we are willing and obedient to change.

We know that abuse (physical, emotional, and psychological), infidelity (cheating and being sexually unfaithful), anger, wandering eyes (looking and flirting), and other negative emotions, neglect, money problems, and substance abuse, among other things, can bring a marriage to an abrupt end. Without going into the proper medical side of things, all abuse is bad and not acceptable, and we know that it does happen. Certain demeaning words used regularly can tear down, manipulate, hurt, and weaken a person's ability to think straight. This abuse is not physical but psychological, and it happens in homes where people profess to know and love the Lord. Even in the best of marriages, misunderstandings and conflicts are inevitable. We all sometimes ere in what we call JAW, judgement, actions, and words. JAW is our acronym for **hasty judgments**, **thoughtless actions**, or **hurtful words**. These negative behaviors can erode the foundation of a long-lasting relationship. That is why it is crucial to be mindful of these pitfalls and to work together to overcome them, cultivating a strong and healthy connection built on mutual respect and understanding.

It is important to clarify that marriage is not just a formal ceremony or a legal document. It is a sacred commitment between two people who are dedicated to building a life together. While some may argue that living together or having a causal relationship is equivalent to marriage, this perspective fails to recognize the spiritual and emotional significance of this union. Friends with benefits (FWB) is not marriage. Celebrities or public figures who glamorize these alternative lifestyles have contributed to a cultural shift away from Godly values, but that does not make them morally or spiritually acceptable. From a biblical standpoint, God created man and woman to unite in a sacred union that honors and glorifies Him. Approaching marriage with the right mindset and intentions is crucial. We should revere and respect it, recognizing its potential to bring joy, fulfillment, and abundance to our lives.

Marriage is a complex relationship that requires effort from both partners. It involves cooperation, and mutual respect. It is like a two-way street, where both people must be willing to yield and make adjustments to keep the peace. Marriage is like a garden which needs to be cultivated, and requires plenty of water, light, and continuous care so it will not fail and be overtaken by weeds and pests. But, also like a garden, marriage will also fail when there is a lack of light, dryness, and up-and-down care. We understand that many men and women face marital challenges, and we extend our support and empathy to them. Keep pushing forward, even if the journey is complex and the road seems long. Remember that there is always a bright side, even if it leads to separation or divorce, to retain peace.

Here is a little history lesson. In Congress, on July 4, 1776, the Declaration of Independence was ratified and signed by fifty-six men. The preamble, "We hold these truths to be self-evident, that all men are created equal, that they are endowed by their Creator with certain unalienable rights, that among these are Life, Liberty and the Pursuit of happiness." 'These stirring words were designed to convince Americans to put their lives on the line for the cause. Separation from the mother country threatened their sense of security, economic stability, and identity. The preamble sought to inspire and unite them through the vision of a better life.'" ("The Declaration of Independence: What Does It Say? | National Archives").

Now, you are wondering why the reference to the Declaration of Independence is in a book about marriage and staying power. The thirteen states of America united and sought a separation from the King of Great Britain, King George III, and no longer wanted to continue in servitude. It became necessary for the thirteen states to unite and declare the causes of their separation. As the fifty-six men declared a litany of valid complaints against King George III, and sought their independence, husbands and wives should similarly discuss the causes leading them to a separation. When couples communicate and address complaints, reconciliation and change can occur, or separation may be inevitable. When a long train of abuses, breach of trust, cruelty, domination, or lack of empathy continues, we do have the right to alter or terminate a marriage and pursue life, liberty, and happiness. Especially if the dynamics of the relationship have changed from one where the other person was supportive, defensive, and had your best interests at heart to one where they are neglectful and even hostile towards you. However, we do understand that you may not want to dwell on separation any longer. The history lesson is over! Just a thought. Moving on...

Unfortunately, many marriages fail because one partner seeks control. Even Christian marriages are not immune to these difficulties. In our experience, there are four common reasons why marriages fail: poor communication, financial problems, a lack of sexual intimacy and fulfillment, and unhealthy relationships. Addressing these issues can be challenging, but with effort and dedication, couples can work through them and build strong, lasting marriages.

Understanding these four major keys that tie into a long-lasting marriage gives you the power to stay in a loving and committed marriage relationship. Successful relationships rely on effective communication. When done correctly, communication can lead to understanding and agreement, but when done poorly, it can result in disagreements and misunderstandings. Spending money wisely is crucial, as it is important to avoid both overspending and being too frugal. Sex is a complex topic and can evoke a wide range of emotions. It is natural to ponder if you are satisfied or frustrated. When evaluating a troubled relationship, it is important to determine if you and your partner view your marriage as a partnership or as a sole proprietorship. Power dynamics in a marriage are not solely gender based. It is not always the man who wants control in the relationship. There are women who thrive on control, too. Hostility can flow freely in both directions of the relationship. Remember that regardless of gender, marital problems can arise due to issues with communication, finances, intimacy, and overall relationship dynamics. These difficulties can lead to divorce or present an opportunity for growth and resolution. It is important to avoid using factors such as age, status, job title, or income to control your partner in the relationship.

We can overcome struggles and adversities in marriage if we remember the things that the Lord has spoken to us, in John 16:33, that in him we might have peace. Tribulation is a part of the world, but we can be of good cheer because Jesus have overcome the world. John 10:10, The New International Version (NIV) says, *"The thief comes only to steal and kill and destroy;"* and the thief, the enemy in marriage is Satan, and he comes to steal your joy, kill your testimony, and destroy your life and marriage. But Jesus said in the latter part of verse 10, *"I have come that they may have life, and have it to the full."* So, in Christ we can be of good cheer.

If you are looking to build a successful and long-lasting marriage, *Staying Power - Four Keys to a Long-Lasting Marriage* is an excellent resource. This book gives practical advice to follow before marriage and throughout your marriage to make it long-lasting, even if it is now in a state of disrepair. By reading this book, you will gain valuable insights into what makes a marriage work, and you will be equipped with the practical tools and knowledge needed to build a strong and healthy relationship with your marriage partner. Once you have read it, consider passing it along to someone else, or buying a copy for someone who may benefit from its wisdom and guidance.

Chapter 1: The First Ordained Marriage

"And the Lord God said, It is not good that the man should be alone; I will make him an help meet for him" (Genesis 2:18). *"So the Lord God caused the man to fall into a deep sleep; and while he was sleeping,* **he took one of the man's ribs and then closed up the place with flesh. Then the Lord God made a woman from the rib he had taken out of the man, and he brought her to the man** (Genesis 2:21-22, and verse 25 (NIV), *"Adam and his wife were both naked, and they felt no shame."*

The Lord God instituted the first marriage union between Adam and Eve, which was good! God intended marriage to be a lifelong commitment, and Adam and Eve did not have to worry about many modern-day challenges that couples face, such as dating, engagement, wedding planning, or in-laws. God saw that it was not good for man to be alone, so he created a helper for Adam. In Genesis 2:23, Adam declared Eve was "*bone of my bones, and flesh of my flesh: she shall be called Woman, because she was taken out of Man.*" Although they faced many challenges throughout their lives, the initial challenges of marriage were not among them, but communication may have been an issue. In Genesis 2:16-17, before God created Eve, He told Adam not to eat of the tree of the knowledge of good and evil, and that if he did eat, death would surely follow. Adam may have been so excited about having Eve that he may not have communicated the weight of not following God's command to her. Nonetheless, when she heard the voice of the serpent saying "Ye shall not surely die," she listened to his communication and not the voice of God.

Miscommunication is always a detriment. How couples manage challenges in their marriage can determine whether their union will be strong and lasting or weak and broken. The institution of marriage has always been a part of God's plan for humanity. It was designed to provide companionship, support, and the opportunity to reproduce. Despite this, humans have often deviated from God's plan and produce their own ideas about marriage. The Bible teaches us that even the Pharisees tried to test Jesus by asking him about divorce.

In Matthew 19:1-12, Amplified Bible (AMP), verses 3-6 says, *"And Pharisees came to Jesus, testing Him and asking, "Is it lawful for a man to divorce his wife for just any reason?" He replied, "Have you never read that He who created them from the beginning made them male and female, and said, 'For this reason a man shall leave his father and mother and shall be joined inseparably to his wife, and the two shall become one flesh'? So they are no longer two, but one flesh. Therefore, what God has joined together, let no one separate."* In verse 8, Jesus made it very plain that Moses only allowed a writing of divorcement because of the hardness of their hearts, and he told them that it was not so in the beginning. *"He said to them, "Because your hearts were hard and stubborn Moses permitted you to divorce your wives; but from the beginning it has not been this way."*

There have been studies that suggest that a significant percentage of "Born Again Christians" may face divorce at some point in their lives. However, it is important to remember that everyone's circumstances are different, and we should not judge or condemn those who have experienced, or will experience divorce. Instead of emphasizing divorce, this book encourages couples to remain committed to each other and work together to create a strong and long-lasting union. It is about recognizing that marriage is a sacred covenant that should not be taken lightly and that we should do everything we can to keep together what God has joined unless He directs us otherwise.

In short, God created the first ordained marriage union. He created a help meet for Adam when He saw that man was alone, Genesis 2:18. God created the male and the female, put them together, and made them one. He took the rib from Adam, created Eve, and brought her to him. To note, in Hebrew, the words "help meet" are two words "Ezer Kenegdo." Ezer means helper and it does not mean one who is subordinate or inferior, but it is used only of a superior or an equal. Ezer Kenegdo means "helper" suitable or comparable" (Benner). Ezer also means to rescue and to be strong. God made Eve for Adam. According to the Bible, when God created Eve, she was intended to complement Adam perfectly. She was his equal and opposite, yet also his helper and support. The Bible says that she was created from one of Adam's ribs, symbolizing that she was a part of him and intended to work alongside him in perfect harmony. This serves as a reminder that each partner is unique in a marriage and brings their strengths and weaknesses to the relationship. By working together and supporting one another, couples can help each other grow and become the best versions of themselves.

The human body has twelve pairs of ribs, twenty-four in total, which protect the vital organs in the chest and abdomen. When God created Eve from one of Adam's ribs, it may have been a symbolic act that represented the special bond and unity that was to exist between husband and wife. By taking one of Adam's ribs, God was creating a partner for Adam and symbolizing the importance of protection and support in a marriage. Just as the rib cage protects the heart, lungs, and other vital organs, Eve was created to protect Adam's heart and provide him with the support and companionship he needed. Together, they were one, united in body and spirit to fulfill God's plan for their lives.

"And God saw every thing that he had made, and, behold, it was very good. And the evening and the morning were the sixth day" (Genesis 1:31).

With Eve, Adam could work together, and they could reproduce and have children. Although the bible does not say how old Eve was, it does say that Adam lived 930 years. Their marriage was until death.

Eve was Adam's everything.

- She was bone of his bone and flesh of his flesh.

- She was his companion.

- She was his helper.

- She was his friend.

- She was suitable for him.

- She was his spouse.

- She was his lover.

- She was the mother of all living.

- She was his wife.

In a healthy and happy marriage, both partners play a vital role in protecting and supporting one another. The story of Adam and Eve makes clear that men and women were created equally with unique qualities that complement each other. Eve was not inferior to Adam, but rather an integral part of him and his partner in life. Together, they were a team, and each brought their own strengths and weaknesses to the relationship. By working together and supporting each other, they were able to fulfill God's plan for their lives. This story is not a myth but rather a reminder of the importance of mutual respect, support, and love in a marriage. If you are willing to put in the effort, your marriage can be rewarding and long-lasting, just as God intended it to be. You were created for success in your marriage, and with God's help, you can achieve it.

Now, we will look at some of the dating and pre-marriage issues of today that can affect a marriage.

Chapter 2: Pre-Marriage

As we explore the topic of pre-marriage, our goal is to strengthen marriages and family life through the examples we share and the pitfalls we caution against. We believe that the lessons learned during the pre-marriage period can be a determining factor in the longevity of a marriage. It is worth noting that while more than seventeen types of marriages are mentioned by different sources on the internet, they are not all ordained by God. Therefore, we are solely focusing on heterosexual, monogamous marriages between one man and one woman. We are not discussing asexual, bisexual, pansexual, or any other type of marriage.

If you are considering marriage, the dating stage is where it all begins. However, before emotions and feelings get involved, it is important to know the person you are entering a relationship with. Make an effort to understand their beliefs and actions. People are becoming more open and expressive with who they are mentally, physically, and spiritually. This is why asking yourself these questions before committing to a relationship is important.

- First, are they John or Jane or are they Eve or Steve? No disrespect to the names mentioned above – used only to correlate whether the person is a male or a female who acts differently from their God-given gender. If so, **RUN**. Consider all things.

- Second, have you seen Dr. Jekyll versus Mr. Hyde mood swings? Is the person well respected and intelligent, yet with a self-absorbed alter ego (narcissistic)? Are they just self-centered? Do they think more highly of themselves than they ought to think? Do they need to be always admired? Are they arrogant? Do they feel that others are inferior to them? And do they have a lack of empathy for others? Do they have a controlling personality? Are they up one day, telling you they love you and throwing insults and attitudes the next day? Do they keep bringing up past incidents? If so, **RUN**. Think about the answers.

- Third, have you experienced a Bruce Banner transformation into the Incredible HULK pattern? When the person is emotionally stressed or pushed to do something outside of their will, do they get angry and unleash rage? Do they also become another individual? Are they messy and do not think they should clean up after themselves? If so, **RUN**.

If you see any of these tendencies, do not go down a road that may lead to heartache and loneliness.

Now that you have pondered these things, let us move on into the dating stage.

A. Dating–Communication: Understanding Through Interaction

It is crucial to take the time to get to know the person you are interested in during the dating stage. This involves observing their attitudes, thoughts, habits, values, and mannerisms. Dating is an opportunity to gather important information about your potential partner and decide if you are compatible. By keeping an open mind and paying attention to what is before you, you can learn much about the person you are dating and make an informed decision about your future together.

Here are five things to learn about your friend, boyfriend (fiancé) or girlfriend (fiancée). As you read this information, you may think of your own questions.

i. **Attitudes** reflect how one thinks, feels, and behaves concerning a situation, person, or thing. The way one acts as a standard or norm. This also relates to behavior. Are they bullies? Do they have a "me first" mentality?

ii. **Thoughts** are ideas or opinions one thinks on. Are the other person's thoughts and opinions usually negative? Do they mention old events repeatedly, even though you thought they were resolved? Do they have a positive outlook or a negative one?

iii. **Habits** are things done regularly, and practices, which can be hard to give up. Is the other person set in their way? Does the other person indulge in things you are not comfortable with? Do they watch movies or TV programs that are demonic, sexual, or profane? Have you heard them speak vulgar language? Do they smoke, drink alcohol, or indulge in mind-altering drugs, even though they may be legal in man's eyes?

iv. **Values** (virtues) show what one considers important and worthwhile. Does the other person's life reflect a life lived in Christ? Does the other person respect their parents and home life? Does the other person value you and your thoughts? Does the person devalue others? Are they demeaning? Do they always push others to do things for them, instead of doing it themselves?

v. **Mannerism** reflects the way one speaks or acts and the methods they use, their ways. Do they speak too roughly or deal harshly with other people? Does the other person always want to be in control? Have you seen another side of your friend that causes a second thought about them?

The dating stage can be a thrilling and enjoyable experience, or it can be stressful and exhausting. Regardless of your experience, it is important to use this time to assess the person you are dating and determine whether they are a good fit for you. It is better to learn about any potential red flags or dealbreakers now rather than later. Pay attention to your interactions with them and with others to evaluate whether they are positive or negative. What is in a person will eventually come out them.

Being attentive and observant can help you make an informed decision about your future with a prospective partner. If one individual is all about self in the dating stage, then walk slowly through this time and consider if this is the way you want to live. Small areas of concern can lead to bigger problems later. Pay close attention to their attitudes, thought processes, habits, values, and mannerisms. Are there signs of jealousy? Are they possessive? Are they controlling? Are they super-sensitive? Are they indecisive? Are they over-confident? Becoming too attached too quickly can cause tunnel vision, and you may miss signs of trouble. In 1968, Ray Charles and Jimmy Holiday wrote the song "Understanding." Ray Charles said that understanding was the best thing in the world, and that it was a mighty powerful thing. The message of the chorus was great, but Ray Charles took the lyrics to a dark place. That is not where we are going with the chorus. Our only message today is to declare that understanding is a beneficial factor and needed in the world.

Understanding the person with whom you want to share your life with is first. If you are dating intending to get married and want your marriage to have staying power, remember that *"wisdom is the principal thing; therefore get wisdom: and with all thy getting get understanding."* Proverbs 4:7. Before deciding on your future with someone, it is important to understand how they communicate with you and others. By taking the time to get to know the person and evaluating how they interact with others, you can determine whether they align with your values and are someone you could see yourself building a long-term relationship with. The goal of the dating stage is to make a well-informed decision about the future of your relationship with an individual.

Now let us look at understanding how they manage their finances.

B. Dating – Financial: Understanding Finances

When it comes to finances, the first step is to evaluate a person's employment status and work ethic. This means finding out if they have a job, if they can keep a job, and if they have the motivation to work to support themselves. Financial stability is an essential factor to consider when entering a long-term relationship because it is vital to ensure that both partners can financially contribute to the household, unless you both agree on only one person working. By having an honest conversation about employment and finances early in the relationship, you can avoid misunderstandings and ensure that you are both on the same page. Be very observant about how the person manages money. A lack of understanding in this area can explode into something more damaging in a marriage. Unfortunately, we have seen this in the lives of people we know. We will briefly address financial difficulties versus financial eases.

Financial Difficulties – A person who shows stress about debt, hardship in paying bills, constant borrowing, out-of-control spending, or credit cards at the maximum level may send a clear message and foreshadow things to come. When you hear things like: "I don't care about the cost, but I must have it; I will double up on my payments later; I will borrow some money from my parents, credit union, etc.; I will use my tithe this time and pay it back later, or I am tired of not getting the things I want." These are areas to discuss and be on one accord with before marriage. Think things over carefully.

Financial Eases – A person who is not drowning in debt, is self-sufficient, pays bills on time, is careful with spending, and is a person who shows that they are dependable and responsible in this area. Our income was particularly good when we met in 1970 at the United States Postal Service, where we both started to work on the same day. We were not in debt, so we felt great about our finances. Maurice was self-sufficient and had his own apartment. I lived at home with my mom but was looking for my own apartment as well.

While Maurice was paying for his apartment, I paid for my tuition at the Washington Technical Institute (now the University of the District of Columbia). We also spent money on alcohol and drugs. Yes, we wasted money and polluted our bodies. During that time, we had no idea that we were fearfully and wonderfully made, and that our bodies were the temple of the living God. We did not know 2 Corinthians 6:16-18, *"And what agreement hath the temple of God with idols? for ye are the temple of the living God; as God hath said, I will dwell in them, and walk in them; and I will be their God, and they shall be my people. Wherefore come out from among them, and be ye separate, saith the Lord, and touch not the unclean thing; and I will receive you. And will be a Father unto you, and ye shall be my sons and daughters, saith the Lord Almighty."*

We both had level heads about finances and respected each other's ideas about spending and paying bills. Finances were not a problem, but we did other things that brought dishonor to the temple of the living God. Moving forward, we further polluted our bodies in matters meant only for the marriage bed. Yes, it was sex before marriage.

C. Dating – Sexual Integrity: Understanding Your Body

Maintaining sexual integrity is an important aspect of taking care of our bodies, and it is especially crucial during the dating stage. While spending time together and building a connection is a natural part of dating, avoid compromising situations that could negatively impact your physical and emotional health.

Let us make it plain, with all the closeness and repeated statements of "I love you," "you make me feel so good," and all the hugs and kisses, you must understand that the flesh will rise. The temptation to commit a wrongdoing (sexual sin, fornication) is certain to occur. Resist the urge to let your emotions and feelings pressure you into doing something that goes against your values and beliefs. Making a mistake and compromising your sexual integrity is not an accident. Take responsibility for your actions rather than making excuses. Own up to your mistakes and work to make things right. No extenuating circumstances can make you fail in your love for honesty, purity, and relationship with the Lord. The dating process should be easygoing and not stressful.

Do you feel delighted or stressed and under pressure? When you enjoy being together with someone, it should always be a delight. Integrity is a choice, so always remember to choose it. Keep honesty, truth, and honor at the front of your relationship, because your decisions define who you are and what you believe in. Keeping secrets, being dishonest, and not respecting time or values can lead to stress and tension. Sexual tension can result in yielding to the thoughts and desires of the other person, and you may fall into the temptation of living together outside of marriage – "common law," or a FWB situation. This is fornication. I Corinthians 6:17-19 (AMP) says, *"But the one who is united and joined to the Lord is one spirit with Him. Run away from sexual immorality [in any form, whether thought or behavior, whether visual or written]. Every other sin that a man commits is outside the body, but the one who is sexually immoral sins against his own body. Do you not know that your body is a temple of the Holy Spirit who is within you, whom you have [received as a gift] from God, and that you are not your own [property]?"* We were bought with the precious blood of Jesus, and we are a part of Him, so honor and glorify God with your body.

The Lord does not approve of any of these situations. Surrendering yourself to sexual sin before marriage can lead to other problems. Sexual sins do not just happen with unbelievers, but they occur with believers as well. Do not let your fleshly desires take control of you through viewing pornography of any form, because what you allow through the eye gate can form your opinion and skew your perspective on real life and sexual intimacy with your spouse. It is a sin, and it is an addiction. Galatians 5:16-17 (NIV) says, *"walk by the Spirit, and you will not gratify the desires of the flesh. For the flesh desires what is contrary to the Spirit, and the Spirit what is contrary to the flesh. They are in conflict with each other, so that you are not to do whatever you want."* In most cases, pornography sins against women and exploits a women's body, but women can also be the initiator of the sin of watching pornography. It is sin, perversion and it promotes violence. Stay free, my friends, and do not fall into sin.

When we were growing up, our parents did not feel comfortable talking about sex or relationships, and we do not blame them for that. Our parents taught us many things and they were good parents, but sex was not a subject of discussion. We had no one to converse with or offer us spiritual guidance on what God's will was for our lives. It was basic knowledge that we should not be doing things that were a part of marriage; however, we allowed our lustful desires to take control and indulged in those things. We knew it was not right, but we gave in to our feelings. We were accountable and without excuse. After accepting Jesus Christ as our personal Lord and Savior, we realized that we had done many things outside of His will for our lives.

At that time, we did not know God's Word or His will. In Hebrews 13:4 (NIV), we later learned that *"Marriage should be honored by all, and the marriage bed kept pure, for God will judge the adulterer and all the sexually immoral."* Our promiscuity went against His will. We believed that we were strengthening our relationship, but we were not, and we did not know what Paul said in Romans 12:1, *"I beseech you therefore, brethren, by the mercies of God, that ye present your bodies a living sacrifice, holy, acceptable unto God, which is your reasonable service."*

D. Dating – Building a Relationship: Understanding the Connection

When you are dating, it is an opportunity to learn more about each other, establish a connection, and find out if you share common interests and values. This is the ideal time to decide whether you can relate to each other, whether you are in sync, and if you can exchange thoughts and experiences to grow closer together.

The Lord has blessed us in our marriage, and we are still celebrating 53 years later. We have had challenges, but we have learned many things and grown from our mistakes. Overcoming those mistakes gave us experience, and we have been blessed to share our experiences with others and see unity come into their marriages. BUILD YOUR RELATIONSHIP!

In understanding how to build relationships, we will associate the game "Connect Four" with two of its winning strategies, and <u>HOW NOT</u> to build a relationship. The two main strategies are predicting the opponent's moves and planning multiple moves ahead to use against them. This type of scheme will make building a relationship incredibly challenging, if not impossible. Run if you see these signs of the "Connect Four" strategy in your relationship. Now a little history about the game.

In 1974, Milton Bradley sold the first Connect Four game. "Connect Four is a two-player game with perfect information for both sides, meaning that nothing is hidden from anyone (*because you see everything*). Connect Four also belongs to the classification of an adversarial, zero-sum game, since a player's advantage is an opponent's disadvantage." (Contributors to Wikimedia projects). In game theory, a progressive game, where one player chooses their action before the other chooses theirs, has perfect information if each player, when making any decision, is perfectly informed of all the events that have previously occurred.

When building a relationship with someone, it is important to be open, honest, and straightforward. This creates an authentic connection between two people. Every decision you make should be based on your individual and collective experiences. Honesty should be the foundation of your relationship. Life is full of lessons, and we should use these experiences to grow together rather than using them as leverage against each other. The best strategy for building a strong relationship is to practice showing each other love, honesty, and care. By consistently practicing these values, you will strengthen your relationship over time.

As previously discussed, while using perfect information and the adversarial, zero-sum game strategy may be effective in playing Connect Four, it is not applicable or beneficial when building personal relationships. In building a relationship, focus on open communication, honesty, and mutual respect. These values will help foster a positive and meaningful connection that can stand the test of time. **Run** if you see signs of an intent to use information to take advantage of someone and use it to their disadvantage. The handwriting may be on the wall. In the dating process, if you need to ask someone else whether you should marry your partner or not, this could be a sign that something is not right. Open your eyes. The decision to marry someone should come from your heart and mind, based on your experiences and connection with your partner. The only other opinion you should look for is the Lord's, which should be the first opinion. While it is always helpful to seek advice from trusted friends and family, the final decision should be yours alone. Trusting the Lord and your intuition can help guide you toward the best decision for your future.

The chart below can be helpful if you want to date and eventually get married. Along with the questions that have already been asked, use this chart to guide your discussions and better understand each other's values and goals. If you are already married, this chart can help you to discuss any issues or areas where you may need to make adjustments. However, it is important to recognize that change can be challenging for both partners. If neither person is willing to make adjustments, separation may be necessary.

When planning for marriage or a profoundly committed relationship, ask yourself these questions. Answer honestly. Discuss your answers with each other. This opens communication, and if you are married use this to help make it better.

1.	**How do I communicate with others when I do not agree with them?**	**Select all that apply**
	A. Non-verbal Communication	
	i. Facial expressions I make	
	1 - Smile	
	2 - Wrinkled eyebrows	
	3 - A puzzled look	
	4 - A stone face	
	B. Verbal Communication	
	i. Pitch (Volume highness or lowness of a tone)	
	1 - Raised pitch, angry, upset, or frustrated	
	2 - Raised pitch, excited, happy, encouraged	
	3 - Lowered pitch, sad, bored, monotone	
	4 - Lowered pitch, soft with listening ear	
	ii. Tone – (The way I speak to someone)	
	1 - Curt, short and rude	
	2 - Calm and professional	
	iii. Content – (What I say)	

	1 - Difficult / hard to understand	
	2 - Clear and easy to understand	
	3 - Confusing	
2.	**How Do I Manage Money?**	**Select all that apply**
	A. I am a first partaker to God	
	B. I buy what is needed	
	C. I buy what I want – when I want	
	D. I pay bills on time	
	E. I pay bills when I can	
	F. I am Thrifty, Prudent, Frugal, Careful, Money-wise	
	G. I am a Tightwad, Miser, Penny-pincher, Scrooge, Hoarder	
	H. I seek the input of others in making big financial decisions (friends, parents, spouse, others)	
	I. It is only my opinion that counts when choosing what to buy	
3.	**How Do I Value Sexual Intimacy?**	**Select all that apply**
	A. Sex is for the marriage bed only	
	B. Sexual activity happens whenever I am aroused	

	C. Sex is for my fulfillment	
	D. I am embarrassed to talk about sex	
	E. I have already had a sexual relationship that have formed my thoughts about sex	
	F. I have had a bad experience with a sexual relationship, and I am afraid	
4.	**How Do I Develop My Relationship with Others?**	**Select all that apply**
	A. Spend quality time together talking, eating, exercising, or doing nothing, but together	
	B. Enjoy moments exchanging ideas	
	C. Gain understanding of differences	
	D. Connect with family	
	E. Make godly decisions together	
	F. Honor and respect my father and my mother	
	G. Agree to disagree (No arguing when compromise is not made)	
	H. Others must do what I want to do	

I. I need "Me Time"	
J. I need a Man Cave or Woman Cave	
K. I want to start a family	
L. I want to have children – How many	

As we conclude this section of "Staying Power," we have taken a glimpse into the first ordained marriage and pre-marriage practices of today, including the dating stage. It is important to reflect and consider these basics that can contribute to the staying power of a marriage. This process starts on day one and continues throughout the relationship. The power to remain united comes from the Lord, but as humans, we have the ability to destroy it and bring it to an end. Then the Lord will allow for separation when there is no unity, abuse and the relationship has been destroyed. If you are in an untenable marital situation, ask the Lord to move them to another place, so that you can live in peace.

If you are in the dating phase of your relationship, take the time to notice and note things that are happening around you. Dating can be exciting or stressful, and what happens before marriage is key. Is your communication easygoing or stressful? Are there financial challenges? Is there a sexual divide? And can you build a relationship where perfect information of earlier occurrences in life are not being used against you, or you using it against someone else?

In the next part of our book, we will discuss what we have found to be four keys to a long-lasting marriage. A long-lasting marriage is possible when both the husband and wife work together as a team.

PART II: Four Keys to a Long-Lasting Marriage

It is important to note that a prenuptial agreement is not one of the keys to a long-lasting marriage. A prenup is a legal agreement made between two people before getting married that outlines the division of property, assets, and support in the event of divorce or death. "*Prenuptial agreements* have long been used by couples who want to set down the terms of any future divorce before they walk down the aisle." ("Prenuptial Agreement Definition & Meaning - Merriam-Webster"). Now, let us discuss the four keys to a long-lasting marriage.

Since God intended for marriage to be permanent and last until death, a prenup is not in His plan for us. We only hear of prenups when divorce is on the table, but we rarely hear about it when death occurs. Planning with a prenup may mean that you are not planning for a long-lasting marriage, but rather setting clear expectations and boundaries in case of a divorce. Marriage is a "work in process," or a "work in progress," either way, work is involved. These terms are used interchangeably in manufacturing raw materials to finished products or the development of something that is not yet complete. When marriage is in the plan, as we said before, it begins at the dating stage, and different pieces come together with the intent to produce a product that will last (Staying Power).

We will look at what we call the four keys to a long-lasting marriage: communication, money, sex, and relationship. We come from different families and backgrounds, but with determination, we can weather life's storms together in marriage. With Christ as our foundation, we have the strength to stand and the power to overcome.

Marriage holds immense power and unity. Together wonderful things can be achieved.

The Lord gave us the power to stay strong, to soar above the storms in life, and to have a long-lasting marriage. He gave us the same tenacity as the eagles. Eagles mate for life and soar high even through the storms because they use the storm's wind to rise. Use the challenges in your marriage to help you rise to a new viewpoint and strengthen your inner man!

Chapter 3: Key One - Communication

Agreement or Disagreement (Harmony or Conflict)

The first key to a long-lasting marriage is communication. It is the best thing in the world. In communication, there can be agreement or disagreement, which can be easy going or stressful. There are four kinds of communication: verbal, non-verbal, written, or visual. Communication, both verbal and non-verbal, is crucial in marriage. While both forms of communication can effectively convey a message, it is vital to give equal importance to both. Verbal communication involves the words we use to express our thoughts and feelings, while non-verbal communication includes our body language, facial expressions, and tone of voice. Paying attention to both aspects of communication can ensure that messages are conveyed clearly and effectively to your spouse.

God valued the importance of communication. In Genesis 11, the people of the earth were of one language, and they began, through communication, to build a tower to reach heaven and make a name for themselves because they did not want to be scattered throughout the earth. They communicated verbally and non-verbally through their actions. As Genesis 11:6-7 (NIV) says, *"The Lord said, "If as one people speaking the same language they have begun to do this, then nothing they plan to do will be impossible for them. Come, let us go down and confuse their language so they will not understand each other.""* As a result, they stopped building. They stopped working together for a common cause, even though the cause was to make a name for themselves, and to be as a god. To the point, when there is no communication, there is confusion. Positive communication occurs when the intention behind it is right, while negative communication results from wrong intentions.

Using verbal communication to share and exchange thoughts and ideas is a key to a long-lasting marriage. Effective communication in marriage requires both parties to listen to each other without prejudice. Having an open dialogue is impossible if one or both individuals have preconceived notions and opinions. We can create a safe space for open communication and mutual understanding by actively listening without judgment. We can build a stronger foundation of trust and respect when we let go of our biases and truly listen to our partner's words and emotions. In a marriage, it is important to have open discussions about daily events, work, children, and emotions. However, it is important to avoid fixating on one subject for too long and to strive for balance, avoiding repetition and one-sidedness.

Healthy communication involves an even exchange of thoughts and feelings, where both parties share their perspectives and listen to each other. During such times, it is crucial to practice empathy and offer silence, as it can help our partner feel heard and understood. Having compassion and remaining silent during times of need is different from suffering in silence. There are times in marriage when one or both individuals may choose to remain silent for the sake of peace. However, it is important not to make silence a habit. That would make one "Taciturn," habitually silent, reserved, and uncommunicative. Taciturn implies a temperamental disinclination to speech and usually connotes unsociability.

("Taciturn Definition & Meaning - Merriam-Webster"). There are some married people who have suffered in silence due to selfishness, abuse, and miscommunication.

Effective communication is essential for a strong and healthy marriage. It is the foundation that holds the union together, ensuring both partners feel heard, understood, and respected. Like glue binds things together, communication binds the couple's hearts and minds and makes them united. Merriam-Webster says that union: 1a (2) an act or instance of uniting or joining two or more things into one: such as uniting in marriage. ("Union Definition & Meaning - Merriam-Webster")

Communicating with understanding and with peace is always the key to success in a marriage. Uniting, in union and becoming one! Effective communication cannot be achieved through arguing and bickering. It is important to maintain a calm and respectful attitude in order to successfully communicate with each other. We can agree or disagree on things, but our Heavenly Father has given us an example and pattern to follow, and if we do, we will have a successful life, and a long-lasting marriage. If we listen to God and obey His voice, we will be a kingdom of priests, and a holy nation. In Exodus 19:5, God spoke to Moses and told him to tell Israel, *"Now therefore, if ye will obey my voice indeed, and keep my covenant, then ye shall be a peculiar treasure unto me above all people: for all the earth is mine."*

Then in Exodus 20:18-21, during the time that God gave to Moses the Ten Commandments, the children of Israel were afraid to talk with the Lord, because they thought that they would die, because of their sin and wrongdoing. God spoke to Moses on Mount Sinai and gave him the Ten Commandments to share with the Children of Israel. Moses then relayed this information to the people, telling them that God had spoken to him from heaven and instructed them on what to do and what not to do. Moses shared God's commandments with them. The Israelites feared talking to God because they knew they had committed wrongdoings.

It is unfortunate when fear prevents us from communicating with God. He told us to listen and obey. It is sad that in marriage, we become afraid to speak the truth. This can be due to past wrongdoings or simply a fear of the other person's reaction. Sin creeps in when that happens, and the communication breaks down. Strive to keep the lines of communication open with your spouse and with God. It is the best thing in the world. We communicate with God through prayer and communicate with each other by talking. Never be afraid to communicate or to seek help from a Christian counselor who will help you both to make corrections in your communication. Marriages risk failure when one partner refuses to get help or is unwilling to change.

In tense situations, it is possible to agree not to argue a point, even if there is a difference of opinion. This is known as "agreeing to disagree." Talking is the key factor in communication. It is true that when God speaks, we should listen, but it is also important to remember that He allows us to speak to Him through prayer. In Deuteronomy 5:4, the Lord talked to Moses, face to face, and in verse twenty-four, the note is that God talked with man, and they heard Him. We can talk to God and not be afraid. Similarly, we should be able to speak to our spouse and not be afraid. We should never be afraid to communicate the truth, in love with each other. While timing is always important, we should not allow our silence to become an obstacle in achieving a successful marriage.

Texting, emailing, Facebook Messenger, Instagram, Snapchat, Twitter - now X, Reddit, LinkedIn, Google+, YouTube, Pinterest and other 21st-century communication cannot replace the value of talking face-to-face. When face-to-face meetings are not possible, tools like Zoom can be helpful. However, it is important to prioritize in-person conversations whenever possible. Our faces can show excitement, understanding and agreement or frustration, misunderstanding, and disagreement, and this is when non-verbal communication is important because facial expressions and body movements can tell a story. However, there are times when talking face to face brings too much heartache and pain because of a broken relationship.

When there is agreement, there is peace. Even trivial things like the way we put the toilet paper roll on, squeeze toothpaste in the middle of the tube instead of the end of the tube, or leaving the toilet seat up can cause disputes in a marriage. Seek peace and pursue unity. Change can take place when peace is present. You can agree and change, agree to disagree, or remain the same and have problems. But, you must communicate and work together.

Before you come to a point of breakdown, praying together is a key to keeping the lines of communication open with God and with our spouses. Praying together, ten minutes a day, will help you to stay connected and in peace!

Communication is our first key that promotes a long-lasting marriage.

A lack of communication brings separation.

Keep it real. **TALK**.

- Be **T**ransparent and make it plain.

- Be **A**ware of each other's feelings.

- Be **L**istening and caring.

- Be **K**ind and considerate.

Early in our marriage, we experienced a real breakdown in communication, which lasted about a year. Our blissful honeymoon lasted for about three and a half years, then our communication broke down. I was on the quiet side and Maurice, after having been a sergeant in the military, was loud, stubborn and took the offensive position, and patience was not one of his best qualities. I would go silent and would not argue when he got loud. Although my silence may have kept the peace, we should have communicated better. There were times when I would hum a song called "Until then I'll Suffer" by Barbara Lynn. The words of the song, that "someday I would be happy," resonated with me, but until then I would suffer.

Humming was a solace for me, and we struggled in our relationship for a year, but we both knew that change needed to happen.

In a marriage, silence, as a defense does not bring resolution, because there is no communication to agree on. Maurice was the only wage earner for the first four and a half years of our marriage, and the financial pressure took a toll on his patience. We had three children and at times funds were very tight. He was never violent or abusive, and he always made sure that we had a roof over our heads and food to eat. Our differences and my silence did not affect his love and care for me and our children. As I thought about our family and relationship dynamic, I realized that there was a pressing need for improved communication. So, one day, I spoke up without resorting to shouting or profanity. After I expressed my opinion, he became silent and stopped talking. He finally listened and took note that change needed to take place. Whenever we had disagreements, we tried to keep them hidden from our children and kept our voices down, though we were not always successful. During those times when we did not agree, our little ones were listening. Excessive quietness or disturbances can be detrimental to any marriage or relationship and family. Change needed to happen, and we needed to work together to make it happen. No matter what any may say, we knew that God was working in us and our marriage long before we came to know Him. We are grateful to Him for inspiring us to break the silence, loudness, stubbornness, and bickering. After our year of struggle, we reconnected as the friends we used to be and enjoyed each other's company, drinking, smoking, and listening to music that we both liked. This was prior to our accepting Christ as our Lord and Savior.

In November 1978, Maurice repented, accepted Christ, was baptized, and later received the gift of the Holy Spirit. I noticed a significant change in him – a complete transformation. The change was real. I thought that I had lost my best friend again because we could no longer drink or smoke together. He would not go into the liquor store, even to buy me a soda, and that made me mad. When he went to church, I stayed home. It was not until February 1979 that I did what Maurice had done, accepted Christ's finished work, and saving grace, and later received the infilling of the Holy Spirit. Then, I began to understand the song "What A Friend We Have in Jesus." Before then, I always associated the song with my grandmother's funeral, in 1963, and it brought sadness. After my encounter with the Lord, the song took on a new meaning for me. I knew that I had a friend in Jesus and His amazing grace brought us to where we were as individuals and as a couple. The Lord began to change things, then the solace was in knowing that we were children of the Most-High God and with Him all things are possible. My songs changed.

The songs "What A Friend We Have in Jesus," written by Joseph Scriven, music composed by Charles Converse and "Amazing Grace," written by John Newton became my songs of praise. Through the words of these songs, we understood that Jesus is our friend and that He carried the weight and penalty for our sins. We can take everything to God in prayer and have peace. We may have trials, temptations, and troubles, but should never be discouraged. He is our faithful friend! The song, "Amazing Grace" is a sweet, sweet reminder that we were saved by God's amazing grace. His grace brought us through many dangers, hard work, and traps, and will always guide us to home and safety.

We find comfort in the lyrics of these songs because they remind us of the journey the Lord brought us through and His desire for unity among us. One with Him and one with each other. Our communication changed after we accepted Jesus as our Lord and Savior, and we began to discuss things and agree on them. We have not been silent since those early years of marriage. We learned more about God's will for our lives, how to love and honor one another, and we learned much patience. Communication with the Lord and each other is the first key to a long-lasting marriage. It has a lasting impact.

In our next chapter, we will consider the second key to having a long-lasting marriage. Money, money, money. Now, that is a little overkill, but it is important.

Chapter 4: Key Two - Money

Spendthrift or Stingy (Reckless – Tightfisted)

Money, and the handling of it, is our second key that impacts a long-lasting marriage. Money can be a blessing, and it can also bring sorrow. Ecclesiastes 10:19, states that *"money answereth all things."* In a marriage, the issue with money is often less about the lack of it and more about unwise spending habits and poor financial planning. Spending wastefully or recklessly is just as problematic as spending grudgingly or penny-pinching to the point of not supporting your family. When couples work together, they can utilize blessings of money from God to bring financial benefits and strengthen their bond. It brings you and your spouse closer together. Talk about it, pray about it, and if there is a special sale on something you need, agree to purchase it, and strike the iron while it is hot, and always remember that our blessings come from the Lord.

Let us discuss tithing since it can be a major factor in Christian relationships when it comes to money. If one person feels that tithing and giving is being a spendthrift and reckless and the other person considers it to be a blessing and needful, there will be a strain on the marriage and the relationship. These differences of opinion about giving tithes and offerings can lead into arguments, stressful situations and missed benefits that come with giving. We learned about the importance of tithing (giving a tenth) after we surrendered our lives to the Lord. We started giving our tithe and offerings from our gross income, even before paying our bills. This practice has become a priority for us, and it has helped us prioritize our finances and strengthen our faith. During the times when we struggled to make ends meet, we never struggled in our

commitment to worship the Lord in giving of tithes and offerings. We have watched God open doors for us, both financially and non-financially, and He has shut doors that would have caused loss. He has been very faithful to us, and we have been faithful to Him. Luke 6:38 is our continuing practice. *"Give, and it shall be given unto you; good measure, pressed down, and shaken together, and running over, shall men give into your bosom. For with the same measure that ye mete withal it shall be measured to you again."* God is always faithful, and He is always looking out for us. Be faithful in your giving. Do not allow thoughts of withholding your giving to God to hamper your marriage or your blessings. Understand whether your partner has the same perspective on giving and being faithful as you do, because it will be an issue where there is continuing disagreement. Remember Proverbs11:24-25 (AMP), *"There is the one who [generously] scatters [abroad], and yet increases all the more; And there is the one who withholds what is justly due, but it results only in want and poverty.*
The generous man [is a source of blessing and] shall be prosperous and enriched, And he who waters will himself be watered [reaping the generosity he has sown].

Now let us take a look at credit card debt and how improper use of credit cards can lead to many marital issues. Credit card use can easily lead to credit card abuse, and that can break a marriage.

We praise God for His faithfulness to us and remember where He brought us from, through the hardships and the blessings. He met our needs, but we had much to learn, and some through trial and error. One

Christmas, when our girls were young, we did not have any cash, so we used our credit card to buy gifts for them. We had a lot of gifts under the tree, but it took more than four years to pay that debt off. That year, we watched our children play with their gifts and carelessly leaving them scattered on the floor was disheartening, even though we knew our spending was not their responsibility to bear. They were not aware of the fact that we had gone into debt to buy those gifts and that it would take years to repay the bill. We declared that we would never do that again. Our favorite expression was that "money doesn't grow on trees," and "even though our name is 'Banks,' we don't own any banks." Our girls learned to take better care of their things at an early age because we told them that if they did not clean up after themselves, we would take all their toys to the thrift store and give them away to children who would appreciate them. We know that it was a little hard, but teaching our children the value of responsibility and financial management has helped them grow into responsible individuals. Today, we are happy to see that they appreciate our efforts by acknowledging our lessons from time to time. They value money and try to spend it wisely. They understand that credit cards are very needful, and they help to build credit, but they can also be a disadvantage if used unwisely.

Spending money wisely and taking care of our needs is a priority. After being home raising our children, I returned to work, and we made the decision to simplify our bill payment process. We decided to pay all our bills from one checking account, even though both of our accounts were joint accounts. Our aim was to consolidate our finances and bill payment process and truly become one. Well, that was a lesson well learned. While Maurice was skilled in working with his hands and cooking, he struggled with tasks such as math, reconciling bank accounts, and keeping track of multiple checks written in the checkbook. During that time, he forgot to write in the checkbook register, a check that was written for our rent, and ended up writing another check to pay the rent, resulting in double payment of our rent. We did not have any extra money in those days to pay extra, so our stress levels rose significantly, causing a major disagreement between us. After some discussion, we both agreed that the person better at working with numbers would take care of reconciling bank accounts and tracking checkbook transactions. Well, my husband knew I had a natural ability with numbers, so we agreed that I would take over the bill-paying process. We discussed our bills, what money was available to pay them, developed a spending plan, and I ensured that the bills were paid on time, with no duplicates, and accounts reconciled. This has worked for us, and we are happy. We still have joint accounts, but all our monies are visible to each of us, and we agree on bill paying. Transparency plays a vital role in building trust and maintaining open communication between people. It not only helps to establish credibility but also minimizes some money issues. We look back at those days and laugh.

We believe couples should be transparent about finances while being realistic in financial resource management. In marriages where one partner tends to spend too much, hoard money, or hide their purchases, it might be a good idea to opt for separate accounts. Separate accounts can still be a workable option when married people can come to an agreement on how to spend their money, pay bills, and meet their household needs.

Irrational spending can be as problematic as excessively saving and not purchasing necessary items. And, let us make it real plain that spending money on gambling, drugs, and liquor (spirits) is unwise and against God's standards.

During the time of the Covid-19 Pandemic, 2020-2022, we all spent money to stock up on food, and other needful household items like toilet tissue, gloves, bleach, anti-bacterial wipes, and alcohol wipes. Some stores implemented a one or two-item purchase policy per visit to prevent hoarding. This was not the typical way of making purchases, but for some people, it became their routine of constantly buying more. Spending money without considering the consequences can bring a marriage to its knees, and we do not mean on your knees praying. We know of several marriages, including some Christian marriages, where one of the spouses could not control their spending. They sometimes purchased duplicate items due to forgetfulness of prior purchases or storage location. The size of their homes did not cause them to lose the items they purchased, but it was because they had hoarder tendencies. This compulsive buying behavior became a destructive force that caused many arguments, and mistrust, and led some to separation and divorce. Their spending was an issue.

When there is an issue with spending money, it can even become difficult to pay bills on time. Managing credit card payments can be especially challenging, when the minimum payment amount increases as the balance goes up, and there are not enough funds available to meet the requirement.

Whether struggling to pay bills or being a saver, being an obsessive saver is just as detrimental as being tight-fisted (unwilling to spend money). When someone has an abnormal desire to save money, they may be experiencing a "Depression-era mentality", which is a fear of losing what you have. Be aware of these tendencies, as they can be dangerous and lead to negative consequences. We are told in 1 Timothy 6:10 that we should have no love for money. *"For the love of money is the root of all evil: which while some coveted after, they have erred from the faith, and pierced themselves through with many sorrows."*

In 1973, The O'Jays released "For the Love of Money". The song pointed out the wrong uses of money. The song spoke about people who would steal, rob, and lie, and that they would not care who they hurt. They implored people not to let money change them because this is what the love of money would do. Do not love money.

In marriage, when both spouses agree to be responsible for their finances, the Lord will bless and provide for them. Do not splurge on things that can wait until another time. Spend money to take care of yourselves and the needs of your home and family. Saving money is excellent, but letting the roof leak, not fixing the heating unit before winter, or spending on things that are not healthy is not reasonable. Delayed maintenance increases household costs. Spend money when it is a necessity.

Our last thought on money is to always thank God for His bountiful blessings of finances, regardless of whether it is the wife or the husband whose income is the greatest. You are a team. Do not become haughty because you bring home more than your spouse, or do not become angry because you are not getting the raises or awards that your spouse receives. Both of these negative emotions can cause marital problems. Where envy and strife is, there is confusion and every evil work.

When we were working, God blessed us both with awards and promotions, and we cheered each other's successes. We did not and do not allow jealousy and conflict to arise whenever He blesses us financially. We were and are happy for each other!

In our next chapter, we will talk about being aroused and stimulated. We will talk about sex.

(sakepaint)

Chapter 5: Key Three - Sex

Fulfillment or Frustration

Sex is a three-letter word that can immediately cause an intense response. It is a sensitive topic for many people, often causing discomfort or embarrassment. However, sexual intimacy can be a positive and enjoyable experience, while a lack of sexual fulfillment can lead to frustration. It is important to note that sex with your spouse is a way to nurture love and form an emotional connection. Sex can be a slow or a fast dance. The wife may enjoy the slow dance like an exceptionally long beat song "Rainy Night in Georgia" sang by Brook Benton in 1970. Meanwhile, the husband is most likely to jump to the sprint ("Let's Get It On" by Marvin Gaye in 1973). But sex should not be like a racehorse coming out of the gate. This is where verbal communication is necessary to express your fulfillment or your frustration. Change and agreement can happen when you are on the same sheet of music.

We have experienced frustration but learned how to move beyond it to fulfillment. The frustration stemmed from a lack of understanding each other's physical limitations and challenges. However, we learned to avoid exhausting ourselves with chores or running around and instead took time to engage in foreplay. We wanted to have a "Most Excellent Intimate Encounter" (We tagged the acronym MEIE). A little bit of foreplay can make a huge difference in our intimacy. We cherish taking our time to please each other. We express our love and affection for each other all the time with a touch on the ear, a rub on the back, a pat on the buttocks, a kiss, sweet words of affection or just a hug. Non-verbal communication plays an important role in our desire to establish intimacy with each other. It helps to solidify this desire. Guys slow your roll to the grand finale.

Intimacy can decline due to factors like having children or job constraints, but it can be strengthened with nurturing. Intimacy is like a flower that blossoms with each passing day. As we matured in our marriage and age, we recognized that our bodies needed a little help. Erectile dysfunction and vaginal dryness can be frustrating if you let it. We needed a little moisture to avoid friction and make a smooth transition. Do not let static stop you because it is often the enemy, whispering words that fuel anger and a desire to quit. The body can also be challenged and tired. But we have a multitude of weapons! Do not listen to the devil, do not make comments that are not productive, and do not become frustrated. Live for fulfillment. Prepare: shower, shave, brush your teeth and gargle. Set the mood. Agree on the timing. Be flexible if changes need to be made due to unavoidable circumstances.

Sexual intimacy can be fun and there is no one set way to experience it with your spouse. But stay within God's will. You both must agree on how to creatively mix things up. Let us be clear, we are only speaking regarding positions or timing, not things that society says are good. Do not get caught up in watching pornography. It is against God's will. Matthew 5:27-28 (AMP) says, *"You have heard that it was said, 'You shall not commit adultery'; but I say to you that everyone who [so much as] looks at a woman with lust for her has already committed adultery with her in his heart."* Watching pornography is adultery. It is hostility toward mostly women and children, and it is not an option to use to arouse yourself. Express your love and care for each other and stay godly. *"Marriage is to be held in honor among all [that is, regarded as something of great value], and the marriage bed undefiled [by immorality or by any sexual sin]; for God will judge the sexually immoral and adulterous."* Hebrews 13:4 (AMP).

Husbands, love your wives and respect their bodies. After childbirth, give your wife time for her body to restore itself. Do not rush to have sex because it is something you desire. Also remember that your wife's body is open and susceptible to becoming pregnant again. Having too many children born too closely together not only increases the number of mouths to feed but also takes a toll on the mother's body. Savor your waiting time so that your MEIE is fulfilling and enjoyable for both partners. Use your waiting time to assist your wife in baby care and other household duties.

Raising children is not solely the wife's responsibility. Managing childcare and household duties can be challenging, and either spouse may be exhausted from work which can lead to a decrease in intimacy. Reduced intimacy in a marriage can cause issues, such as infidelity and emotional turmoil, and those issues are not acceptable. Therefore, it is crucial to work together to raise your children in a manner that honors God. Fathers should also desire a long and healthy life for their wives as they are equal partners in supporting the family. Communicate and work together.

SEX - **S**avor the experience, **E**njoy the encounter, and use the **X**-ray approach (invisible electromagnetic energy). Why did we say to use the x-ray approach? The x-ray looks through, reveals, and identifies any problems that may arise. Enjoy your MEIE.

Now, work together and see the beauty of partnership in relationships in the next chapter.

Chapter 6: Key Four – Relationship

Partnership or Sole Proprietorship

The fourth key to a long-lasting marriage is a strong relationship. Husbands and wives must maintain a deep connection. Most people connect romance, love or sex when discussing relationships, but that is not the sum. In our marriage, we are equal partners, not a sole proprietorship, where one person controls all or a corporation where multiple people outside of the marriage controls things.

When we were younger, no one taught us about marriage and relationships. We share a marital relationship and a spiritual connection in Christ. Even before we came to the saving knowledge of Jesus Christ, the Lord led us in small ways to do things together. Our family came first, and we did our best to agree and work as one. Our true relationship came to be after we accepted Christ and surrendered our lives to Him. First, we prioritized our relationship with God; then we focused on self-care, marriage, children, and others. Our connection with God taught us to enjoy one another more. We love our partnership!

When two people join in marriage, they blend their time, money, efforts, and lifestyle. It takes time but build on the things that work together for the greater good. We are connected not just by our marriage license but also by creating things together as a single unit. We depend on each other for support and encouragement, which includes uplifting each other's confidence. It is important to express praise and gratitude for the things we do for one another.

When our children were in elementary school, one of our senior Christian neighbors, Mrs. Esther Rudd, spoke a prophetic word and a word of knowledge to us. Although we did not know the ramifications of the words at that time, we received them and considered them. She said that she saw Maurice as a minister, and she encouraged us to build our relationship with each other. Her words were that she could see that we loved and cared for our children, but advised us not to make them the center of our lives, because they would grow up and move on, and our marriage would lack if we did not have a good relationship. Although it took years for our children to grow up and move out, and years before Maurice became a minister of the Gospel, her words came to pass. Our marriage did not lack because we took care of and concern for it. Her words about our children and Maurice were spot on, and her encouragement about our relationship helped us to build unity and take the time to get away and enjoy each other.

Even when our resources were limited, we tried to take a weekend away every three to four months. Maurice's oldest brother, Robert, also encouraged us to take weekend trips together. We went to Howard Johnson's, Holiday Inn, The Red Roof Inn, Best Western, Motel 6, Shenandoah Valley, VA, Williamsburg, VA, Lancaster, PA, and Front Royal, VA. It was great to get away and improve our relationship as a couple.

We had a great relationship despite our different interests, and we understood that doing things separately, most of the time, could cause a break in the relationship. We did not want to become vulnerable and be tempted to do wrong things. We believe that God's goodness encompasses every aspect of our lives. Although there may have been times when we did not understand God's actions or why certain things happened, we refused to allow evil to arise from our independence from God or from each other. My husband and I enjoy spending time together because we have a connection. We are friends, lovers, best buds, and helpers to each other. We show respect and love to one another. We have fun! That does not mean we do not have challenges, because we do, but we remember who called us and whose we are.

We love the Lord and always strive to follow His will. Sometimes, though, we must bite our tongues to maintain peace. No, it is not easy, but possible. Timing is everything. There are times when it is best to remain silent and times when speaking out is necessary. When differences occur, use the blood pressure (BP) lowering concept, which is to breathe through your nose, inflate your chest and hold it a few seconds, and release the air slowly through your mouth. Two things happen when you do this, your BP does lower, and your mind and emotions settle. It is a win-win that will give you a moment to reflect and be at peace. We strive to be sensitive to these situations, adjusting our thoughts and actions accordingly to avoid misunderstandings or conflicts.

When differences of opinion occur between us, we take a moment to reflect before responding, and that has been a great tool in our marriage. Discussing a matter is a part of communication, but it is also a part of building a relationship together. But remember, after a brief moment, always take time to discuss the matter, and <u>do not delay it</u> to another time <u>or ignore</u> the subject. Our differences have blended and made us stronger. In 2024, we celebrated 53 years of marriage, and it is just getting better. We always show our love and appreciation for each other. We share responsibilities, whether it is dealing with finances, cooking, cleaning, washing clothes, or any other task that arises. We are one! This is the Banks Family Partnership!

We have had a partnership from the beginning of our marriage union, even while going through our year of struggle. As previously mentioned, the first four and one-half years of our marriage, Maurice was the sole provider, but he was always supportive of me. When our girls were young, he helped with bathing them, and as they got older, he took them to orthodontics appointments. The only thing that he would not and could not do was their hair, because he was all thumbs with that. After we came to the knowledge of Christ and began to go to church, he would always cook Sunday morning breakfast while I dressed the girls and did their hair. We were a team. We were connected to each other and our children. We did things together. When you saw one of us, you saw all of us. Our church friends called us a troop or a train for always being together. Our troop marched on.

Although we had challenges, our relationship flourished over time, but despite our connection, there were voices in our heads that tried to drive us apart. Every person has three voices that we can choose to listen to, our own voice, our Lord and Savior's voice and the enemy of our soul's voice (Satan). We must choose the right voice. When we did not know the Lord or understand His will for our lives, we listened to ourselves and the enemy. We made decisions and choices that led to more problems, but things changed after we surrendered our lives to the Lord.

When people make choices based on their thoughts or the enemy's voice, it leads to loss. To avoid loss, we must listen to God's voice and align our thoughts to His. The voices in your head can result from emotional manipulation, harsh language, jealousy, anger, betrayal, or doubt. And do not allow the enemy's voice to trap you into thinking that you are married to a good man or a good woman, when the history of manipulation and trauma keeps repeating itself. If a person's actions manifest their inner voice, then those actions reflect their true character. Wake up and see the handwriting on the wall. Remember, that change must happen in both parties for a successful relationship.

If change is not initiated, the four keys to a long-lasting marriage can take a toll on a relationship, but in the reverse. During the tough times in our relationship, we noticed that it all began with a lack of communication, financial problems, and a decrease in sexual intimacy. This led to further problems such as anxiety, emotional distance, anger, and even thoughts of breaking up. We realized that we had been treating our marriage like a sole proprietorship, instead of a partnership, with both of us more focused on our individual satisfaction instead of working together to make things better.

Marriage is a partnership that requires the submission of both parties to the Lord. By sharing thoughts, wants, likes, and dislikes, we learn to become one. Unity and peace are essential for any successful marriage and being present for each other is crucial. If there is no harmony in the home, there will be separation, and when separation of heart, mind and body takes place, absence and lack begin, then comes conflict. 2 Corinthians 5:7-8 says that "we walk by faith, not by sight," and that we are "willing rather to be absent from the body, and to be present with the Lord." But, in marriage, you must be willing to be present and not absent. Absence destroys relationships and agreement. Do not let your livelihood, your ministry, your hobby, or your recreation cause you to be absent in your marriage. Seek peace and pursue it, so you will have balance and harmony, oneness, and partnership. Spending quality time together is just one way to enhance a relationship.

When two individuals enter a marriage, they may have differences, but engaging in activities together can strengthen the bond and narrow the differences. Maurice liked fishing and exercising, and I did not, so even though I had to wear gloves to put the worms on the hooks, I went fishing with him. It was a time for togetherness, and the journey to our destination was an opportunity to bond. And, when he exercised, I joined him. I loved football, and during the years of 1975-1979, I worked a concession stand at R. F. K. Stadium, when the Washington Redskins (now Washington Commanders) played. Although Maurice was not a big sports fan he sat with me, and we watched together when football was on television. Now, we share many likes, but it took time and togetherness to come to where we are. It took work, to make it work.

The effort that you make in making your marriage work is like working in an orchard, and to bear fruit, the trees must be always watered, fertilized, pruned, and sprayed. To bear fruit in your marriage, both husbands and wives must cultivate (keep working to improve) the relationship, both must invest themselves and their time. Uproot things that bring harm or disruption. Do not continue to rehearse past disruptive situations (if they are divisive cut them out of the conversation.). As with the "Connect Four" game, perfect knowledge can be used as a weapon. The constant remembrance and rehearsal of past events or misunderstandings can lead to manipulative tactics, draining the life out of your relationship.

When there is no agreement and no peace, your relationship will fail in the same way that weeds will take over your garden or orchard. Someone said that the devil is in the details, and unity is not whenever the devil is present. If you find that the answers to these questions are unsatisfactory, your relationship with your spouse is in trouble. Does my spouse love me? Does he or she try to manipulate me into doing what they want? Do they act like they really love me and shower me with gifts after they have been verbally, mentally, psychologically, or physically abusive? Do they say one thing and do another? These are tactics that destroy relationships in marriage. Do I stay or do I go? Will they ever change?

Change can take place when peace and unity are present, but when manipulation is present, the relationship must be reevaluated. The number of years in a marriage does not make it great, but the quality of years makes the difference. Love is happiness and there is no point in having 10, 15, or 20 years of misery if love is not in it.

Love grows and flourishes with time and much effort. Husbands and wives must work together as partners. We are equal, and we are whole. Together we are 100 percent equal! We work together in unity for the whole. There are multiple types of love, but we will just briefly mention two. Eros love, which is more geared to sexual pleasures and Pragmatic love, is more geared to a relationship that is based on practical concerns. Eros is intense and fulfilling sexually, get what you can, when you can, and get it quick. Pragmatic love is the type of love that endures the challenges, pitfalls, and the demands of marriage. Pragmatic love looks past our age and our sagging bodies, especially when the earth tries to reclaim our bodies. How? Everything in our bodies wants to sag and go lower toward the ground, because it is a part of life, but our spirits are the same. With Pragmatic love, it never fails. Distractions come and go, but love and care remains.

Do not allow distractions to bring in thoughts of 50/50. When that happens, separation and divorce are inevitable. That is what 50/50 says, it is sagging. It says, SPLIT. Relationships break when there is misunderstanding, a lack of communication and a one-sided mentality by either person.

We share this last story to bring attention to a situation that happened to a couple who had a variety of

74

issues going into their marriage. They allowed the desire for physical attraction to bring them together in marriage, but they both had misconceptions pertaining to what the marriage relationship was supposed to be. Even though they married, their problems remained unresolved. This was his third marriage, and he was controlling, and her first, but she was very independent. During their early years of marriage, the wife's mother took ill. The wife took time off to be with her mother in the hospital. She spent her time at the hospital and neglected her husband, and did not communicate with him, or go home, and when she did speak with him, it was curt. While the circumstance of her not being home was honorable, she could have done better to communicate and speak civilly to her husband. On the other hand, her husband had no empathy for what she was going through, and only looked at his physical need. He was pushy and just as outspoken as she was. The communication and the relationship broke. Unfortunately, her mother passed, and their marriage shortly ended in divorce. She became a very bitter woman, and he went on to marry someone else. Their marriage was on a 50/50 basis, and one-sided, but neither of them took advantage of the keys of communication and relationship.

Marriages are ordained by God, but lived here on earth. It is a continuing work in love. Use these four keys to aid you to have a long-lasting marriage: communicate openly, agree on finances, prioritize intimacy, and build your relationship. Stay focused.

Matthew 19:5-7 *"For this cause shall a man leave father and mother, and shall cleave to his wife: and they twain shall be one flesh? Wherefore they are no more twain, but one flesh. What therefore God hath joined*

together, let not man put asunder."

Let the Lord be in control of your marriage!

Rise above the clouds and soar! Look to Him!

"I lift up my eyes to the mountains—where does my help come from? My help comes from the Lord, the Maker of heaven and earth. He will not let your foot slip—he who watches over you will not slumber" Psalm 121:1-3 (NIV).

PART III: Prayer and Scriptures for Marriage

Chapter 7: Prayer for Marriages

(Pray Together - Use each other's name)

For the health of your relationship and marriage, it is vital that you speak life into it. Do not allow the enemy of your souls to bring separation. It takes two to tango, but both partners must be determined to have peace with each other and in their home. Allow the Lord to keep you.

Seek guidance through prayer and scripture if one spouse is not fulfilling God's will. The Lord will hear and answer you, but it is important to keep in mind that His answer may require you to move on from a relationship to find peace. Even if the physical and emotional connection is no longer there, you can still have the love of the Lord for that person. Let peace prevail.

This prayer can bring reconciliation if both partners agree to change. It is specific in some areas and general in others but can be used as a starting point.

Heavenly Father,

You are the God who sits high and looks low. You ordained marriage, and we thank You for it. I thank You for my (*wife / husband —Speak the Name of Your Spouse*).

In Genesis 2:23-25, Adam said that Eve was bone of his bones, and flesh of his flesh. He called her Woman because she was taken out of Man. God said, *"Therefore shall a man leave his father and his mother, and shall cleave unto his wife: and they shall be one flesh. And they were both naked, the man and his wife, and were not ashamed."* Father, we thank You for making us one.

Lord Jesus, we thank You for confirming the unity of marriage. We thank You for our marriage. In Matthew 19:4-6 (The New International Version), You said, *"that at the beginning the Creator 'made them male and female,' and said, 'For this reason a man will leave his father and mother and be united to his wife, and the two will become one flesh'? So they are no longer two, but one flesh. Therefore what God has joined together, let no one separate."*

We thank You for marriages. They are ordained in heaven, but they are lived here on earth. Lord, we pray that we will love each other as You love the church and have given Yourself for it. Let me cherish my wife who is of good understanding, kind and beautiful, and keep him who is evil in his doings away from her. *"In this same way, husbands ought to love their wives as their own bodies. He who loves his wife loves himself"* (Ephesians 5:28, NIV). Lord, I will always love, honor, and reverence my husband, as unto You. In Ephesians 5:30-32, Lord, You relate marriage of a man and his wife to be as the relationship between Christ and the church. Help us to be the examples that You have set, that we will be one together, and one in You. As we are reconciled unto Christ through the blood of His cross, by Him we are reconciled unto peace.

Heavenly Father, we thank You for peace in our home. We are pleased to be in this union of marriage, and we are pleased to be with each other. I will treat my (*__wife / husband —Speak the Name of Your Spouse__*) with respect and proper communication, and <u>he or she</u> will respond in the same way. Help us both, my (*__wife / husband —Speak the Name of Your Spouse__*) and I to be as lights that shine in darkness. We reflect the love that You have for us. We thank You for Your peace in our marriage. Thank You for blessing us to be an example of righteousness unto our children.

We thank You that we have staying power and that we have learned these four valuable keys to having a long-lasting marriage. We thank you for our willingness to communicate civilly with each other, our agreement in how we spend the finances that You have blessed us with, the enjoyment we have as we are continually ravished by our love for each other, and the relationship that has grown over time. We thank You Lord for the unity, love, and peace that we have in our marriage.

We speak life into our marriage, spiritually, emotionally, sexually, financially and in our relationship. Lord, we give you all the praise, honor, and glory!

In Jesus' name, we pray.

AMEN.

Together, you can write your own prayer. Be encouraged!

Chapter 8: Scriptures to Reflect on

I Corinthians 7:4-5 (AMP)

"The wife does not have [exclusive] authority over her own body, but the husband *shares with her*; and likewise the husband does not have [exclusive] authority over his body, but the wife *shares with him*. Do not deprive each other [of marital rights], except perhaps by mutual consent for a time, so that you may devote yourselves [unhindered] to prayer, but come together again so that Satan will not tempt you [to sin] because of your lack of self-control."

Colossians 3:18-19 (AMP)

"Wives, be subject to your husbands [out of respect for their position as protector, and their accountability to God], as is proper *and* fitting in the Lord. Husbands, love your wives [with an affectionate, sympathetic, selfless love that always seeks the best for them] and do not be embittered *or* resentful toward them [because of the responsibilities of marriage]."

Proverbs 31:10-12

"Who can find a virtuous woman? for her price is far above rubies. The heart of her husband doth safely trust in her, so that he shall have no need of spoil. She will do him good and not evil all the days of her life."

Peter 3:1

"Likewise, ye wives, be in subjection to your own husbands; that, if any obey not the word, they also may without the word be won by the conversation of the wives;"

Peter 3:7 "Likewise, ye husbands, dwell with them according to knowledge, giving honour unto the wife, as unto the weaker vessel, and as being heirs together of the grace of life; that your prayers be not hindered."

Ephesians 5:22 and 25...tells wives to

"submit yourselves unto your own husbands, as unto the Lord," and for husbands to "love your wives, even as Christ also loved the church, and gave himself for it."

Colossians 3:14-16 (AMP)

"Beyond all these things put on *and* wrap yourselves in [unselfish] love, which is the perfect bond of unity [for everything is bound together in agreement when each one seeks the best for others]. Let the peace of Christ [the inner calm of one who walks daily with Him] be the controlling factor in your hearts [deciding and settling questions that arise]. To this *peace* indeed you were called as members in one body [of believers]. And be thankful [to God always]. Let the [spoken] word of Christ have its home within you [dwelling in your heart and mind—permeating every aspect of your being] as you teach [spiritual things] and admonish *and* train one another with all wisdom, singing psalms and hymns and spiritual songs with thankfulness in your hearts to God."

1 Corinthians 13:4-8a (AMP)

"Love endures with patience *and* serenity, love is kind *and* thoughtful, and is not jealous *or* envious; love does not brag and is not proud *or* arrogant. It is not rude; it is not self-seeking, it is not provoked [nor overly sensitive and easily angered]; it does not take into account a wrong *endured*. It does not rejoice at injustice, but rejoices with the truth [when right and truth prevail]. Love bears all things [regardless of what comes], believes all things [looking for the best in each one], hopes all things [remaining steadfast during difficult times], endures all things [without weakening]. Love never fails [it never fades nor ends]."

Scriptures Used in the Book:

Genesis 2:7, 16, 17, 18, 21, 23, 24, 25 - Ephesians 5:30-33

John 16:33 - John 10:10 - Matthew 19:1-12 - Genesis 1:31

Proverbs 4:7 - 2 Corinthians 6:16-18

I Corinthians 6:17-19 - Galatians 5:16-17

Hebrews 13:4 (NIV and AMP)

Romans 12:1 - Genesis 11:6-7 - Exodus 19:5

Exodus 20:18-21 - Deuteronomy 5:4 - Ecclesiastes 10:19

Luke 6:38 - Matthew 5:27-28 - 1 Timothy 6:10

Matthew 5:27-28 - 2 Corinthians 5:7-8

What God has joined together let no man separate.

Conclusion

Genesis 2:7 & 21-24 (NIV)

"Then the Lord God formed a man from the dust of the ground and breathed into his nostrils the breath of life, and the man became a living being." vs. 21-24 *"So the Lord God caused the man to fall into a deep sleep; and while he was sleeping, he took one of the man's ribs and then closed up the place with flesh. Then the Lord God made a woman from the rib he had taken out of the man, and he brought her to the man. The man said, "This is now bone of my bones and flesh of my flesh; she shall be called 'woman,' for she was taken out of man."* That is why a man leaves his father and mother and is united to his wife, and they become one flesh."

God united Adam and Eve as equals despite their challenges. Husbands, love and cherish your wives. They are not inferior or subservient to you but should be respected and honored. Wives, respect and honor your husband, who is not superior or the controller, but the head of the family where God has placed him. If you read anything in this book that indicates the need for change, act now. It may not be too late to save your marriage. If it is "a day late and a dollar short" as they say, or "too little too late," then leave the marriage in peace. As Amos 3:2 says, "Can two walk together, except they be agreed?" Do not make your life any worse.

Staying power is made available and possible by using these four keys. Keep the communication open and honest. Discuss and plan decisions about how and when to spend money. Have fun in sexual intimacy and enjoy. And finally, build your relationship with each other by spending quality time together and with the Lord.

COMMUNICATION

MONEY

SEX

RELATIONSHIP

Bibliography

BibleGateway.com: A searchable online Bible in over 150 versions and 50 languages. (n.d.). Retrieved at various times, from BibleGateway.com: A searchable online Bible in over 150 versions and 50 languages. website: http://www. biblegateway.com

The King James Version present on the Bible Gateway matches the 1987 printing. The KJV is public domain in the United States.

New International Version (NIV)

Holy Bible, New International Version®, NIV® Copyright © 1973, 1978, 1984, 2011 by Biblica, Inc.® Used by per- mission. All rights reserved worldwide.

Amplified Bible (AMP)

Copyright © 2015 by The Lockman Foundation, La Habra, CA 90631. All rights reserved.

"The Declaration of Independence: What Does It Say? | National Archives." *National Archives*, 24 Mar. 2016, https://www.archives.gov/founding-docs/declaration/what-does-it-say .

Benner, Jeff A. "What Is a 'Help Meet?' | AHRC." *The Ancient Hebrew Research Center*, https://www.ancient-hebrew.org/studies-interpretation/what-is-a-help-meet.htm.

Contributors to Wikimedia projects. "Connect Four - Wikipedia." *Wikipedia, the Free Encyclopedia*,

Wikimedia Foundation, Inc., 11 Aug. 2003, https://en.wikipedia.org/wiki/Connect_Four.

Contributors to Wikimedia projects. "Perfect Information - Wikipedia." *Wikipedia, the Free Encyclopedia*, Wikimedia Foundation, Inc., 19 Sept. 2003, https://en.wikipedia.org/wiki/Perfect_information.

"Prenuptial Agreement Definition & Meaning - Merriam-Webster." *Merriam-Webster: America's Most Trusted Dictionary*, https://www.merriam-webster.com/dictionary/prenuptial%20agreement.

"Taciturn Definition & Meaning - Merriam-Webster." *Merriam-Webster: America's Most Trusted Dictionary*, https://www.merriam-webster.com/dictionary/taciturn.

"Union Definition & Meaning - Merriam-Webster." *Merriam-Webster: America's Most Trusted Dictionary*, https://www.merriam-webster.com/dictionary/union.

sakepaint. "Silhouette Of Swan Couple In Love With Heart Shape On Sunset Bridge Lake Stock Photo - Download Image Now - IStock." *IStock*, https://www.istockphoto.com/photo/silhouette-of-swan-couple-in-love-with-heart-shape-on-sunset-bridge-lake-gm985635494-267399340?searchscope=image%2Cfilm.

Acknowledgments

We thank each other for allowing the Lord to use us to be honest, able to share a part of our story, and to be a blessing.

We thank our daughters Rosita Banks-Taylor, Consuela Banks, and Juanita Banks, who have watched us mature as we worked through our growth processes and became one. We are immensely proud parents of who they have become through the values and examples that we have lived and set before them. A special thanks to Juanita for her talents and graphic design of our book cover. And, thanks to Vivian for pictures captured through the years.

We thank the Lord for our spiritual leaders, who have all been a part of our walk with the Lord:

Bishop Jonathon Earl Zeigler II (National Church of God – Our Current Pastor) - Special thanks for his very needful and timely messages about the dynamics of family unity.

Pastors Stephen L. and Janice Lowery (National Church of God)

The Late Bishop Thomas Lanier (TL) and Mildred Lowery (National Church of God)

Pastor Harold and Annette Banks (Greater Apostolic Church of Christ)

The Late Bishop Joseph and Roberta Weathers (Holy Temple Church of Christ)

A special thanks to the Late Mrs. Esther Rudd

About the Authors

Elder Maurice and Vivian Banks were born and raised in Washington, DC, and have resided in Maryland since 1982. They began their journey together as they started on the same day of employment for the United States Postal Service. They are people who have grown together since their youth, and have found practical ways to live, love, laugh, and keep the romance and fun in their marriage.

They suffered trials, lived through drugs and alcohol, and have learned to navigate through them and keep unity in their marriage. They do not always agree on everything, but they do agree to disagree. They work together. After coming to know the Lord, they trust in Him for who He is and what He continues to do in their lives. Their communication, agreement in how they spend their money, sexual intimacy, their relationship, and their prayer life together keeps them in peace.

After many years of praying together, Vivian authored and published "My Little Book of Everyday Prayers (2020), which has been a blessing to many people. Prayer and agreement has given their marriage power to stay in harmony.

They are immensely proud of their daughters and grandchildren. Their time together is always filled with laughter and joy. They make each other laugh, and they appreciate the knowledge, talents, and abilities they all possess. Although Maurice and Vivian are not perfect, they have set a standard of marriage for their family.

Made in the USA
Columbia, SC
22 August 2025

61685824R00050